HUMPBACK WHALES

by Victor Gentle and Janet Perry

Gareth Stevens Publishing
A WORLD ALMANAC EDUCATION GROUP COMPANY

Please visit our web site at: **www.garethstevens.com**
For a free color catalog describing Gareth Stevens' list of high-quality books and
multimedia programs, call 1-800-542-2595 (USA) or 1-800-461-9120 (Canada).
Gareth Stevens Publishing's Fax: (414) 332-3567.

Library of Congress Cataloging-in-Publication Data

Gentle, Victor.
  Humpback whales / by Victor Gentle and Janet Perry.
    p. cm. — (Whales and dolphins: an imagination library series)
  Includes bibliographical references and index.
  ISBN 0-8368-2882-8 (lib. bdg.)
    1. Humpback whale—Juvenile literature. [1. Humpback whale.
  2. Whales.] I. Perry, Janet, 1960- II. Title.
  QL737.C424G46   2001
  599.5'25—dc21   2001020013

First published in 2001 by
Gareth Stevens Publishing
A World Almanac Education Group Company
330 West Olive Street, Suite 100
Milwaukee, WI 53212 USA

Text: Victor Gentle and Janet Perry
Art direction: Karen Knutson
Page layout: Victor Gentle, Janet Perry, Joel Bucaro, and Tammy Gruenewald
Cover design: Joel Bucaro
Series editor: Catherine Gardner
Picture Researcher: Diane Laska-Swanke

Photo credits: Cover © Mark Newman/Visuals Unlimited; p. 5 © Michael S. Nolan/Seapics.com;
p. 7 © Bryan & Cherry Alexander; p. 9 © Brandon D. Cole/Seapics.com; p. 11 © Phillip
Colla/Seapics.com; p. 13 © Amos Nachoum/Seapics.com; p. 15 © Oswaldo Vasquez/Seapics.com;
p. 17 © Doug Perrine/HWRF-NMFS permit #882/Seapics.com; p. 19 © Mark
Carwardine/Seapics.com; p. 21 © James D. Watt/Seapics.com; p. 22 Joel Bucaro/© Gareth
Stevens, Inc., 2001

Printed in the United States of America

1 2 3 4 5 6 7 8 9 05 04 03 02 01

Front cover: A float plane flies dangerously close to a humpback
whale. Weighing about 50,000 pounds (22,700 kilograms), this
magnificent creature has leaped about 30 feet (9 meters) into the air!

TABLE OF CONTENTS

Words that appear in the glossary are printed in **boldface** type the first time they occur in the text.

WE ALMOST WIPED 'EM OUT

Humpback whales have few **predators**. **Orcas** sometimes attack humpbacks and leave teeth marks on their **flukes**. But they rarely manage to kill these powerful giants.

Humans have done much more harm than orcas. After whalers killed 250,000 humpbacks and almost wiped them out, more and more people wanted to save the whales. Finally, in 1966, most nations agreed to stop hunting humpbacks. Unfortunately, a few big whaling nations continued to hunt them.

Since the ban, the number of humpbacks has grown a little. Still, only about 10,000 humpback whales live in our oceans today, compared with hundreds of thousands that lived there a century ago.

A mother and **calf** swim near Hawaii. The most dangerous predators that these giants have faced in their 20-million-year history are humans.

PREDATOR TO PROTECTOR

Like us, whales need air to breathe. Whales drown if they get tangled in fishing nets that hold them underwater.

Some humpbacks are strong enough to stretch the nets and reach the surface, so they can breathe. If they remain stuck in the net, they may still die — unless someone like Jon Lien finds them.

Lien is a Canadian scientist devoted to saving trapped whales. He also helps fishers by freeing the whales gently, with the least possible damage to the nets. Fishers used to kill the whales they found in their nets, and the whales would destroy the nets as they died. Lien wants to teach fishers to become friends of the whales, instead of enemies.

Lien and his team have freed over 1,000 humpbacks from fishing nets off Newfoundland, Canada. Here, Lien uses a hook to untangle a net from a humpback's mouth.

FEARSOME FILTER FEEDERS

Most **cetaceans** have teeth. However, some have **baleen** instead of teeth. Baleen are long, flexible plates that hang from the whale's upper jaw. The edge of each plate has bristles, like a brush.

Humpbacks, like other baleen whales, have huge mouths. To eat, they gulp sea water full of small fish and other tiny sea creatures. They force this lively soup against their baleen. The water squirts out through the baleen, and the creatures are swallowed.

During the long summer, humpbacks eat about a ton of food a day. They have to eat enough to last all year. They do not eat during the winter months, which they spend in their breeding grounds.

You can see baleen plates hanging from this humpback's upper jaw as it gulps fish and water near Alaska. These baleen plates can grow to 3 feet (0.9 m) long.

BLOWING BUBBLES

Humpback whales arrive at their feeding grounds in the spring. For about the next eight months, they focus most of their energy on finding food.

Humpbacks catch their food in a variety of ways. Sometimes, they just open their mouths wide and swim through a **shoal** of fish. Other times, they slap their mighty tails onto the water to stun their **prey**.

Humpbacks have tricks that no other whales use. One trick is the bubble net. Swimming in circles beneath its prey, the humpback lets out a spiral of bubbles. As fish or **krill** swim to the center of the spiral, the whale lunges upward, mouth wide open. Often, the humpback catches a whole shoal this way.

One reason humpback whales blow bubbles is to catch fish. This humpback, however, has a different reason — attracting the attention of a female.

FEEDING OR BREEDING

Humpbacks feed in the cold waters of the far north and far south during spring, summer, and fall. They spend their winters in the warm waters of their breeding grounds, where most **calves** are born.

Midwinter is in December in the northern half of our planet, but in the southern half, December is a summer month. So, while northern humpbacks are busy mating and having calves in tropical waters, southern humpbacks are searching for food near Antarctica.

Humpbacks **migrate** huge distances between their feeding grounds and breeding grounds. They may travel up to 4,000 miles (6,400 kilometers) each way and take up to two months to complete the trip.

Better safe than sorry. This humpback mother in the South Pacific near Tonga swims between her calf and a diver — just in case the diver might be dangerous.

BE MUSIC THE FOOD OF LOVE?

While humpback whales are at their breeding grounds, many of the males sing. The songs may last for just a few minutes or for many hours — even days. All the males from one ocean sing the same beautiful song. Those from another ocean sing a different one. In each group, the song will change over the years.

No one knows why male humpbacks sing. Maybe it is to mark out territory and to warn off other males. Maybe it is to attract female whales. No one knows why the songs change or why all the males seem to learn new tunes at the same time. Humpback whale behavior holds many mysteries.

Humpback males rowdily compete for females in the Silver Bank breeding grounds in the Caribbean Sea. European sailors first saw humpbacks here over 300 years ago.

WE KNOW THEM BY FLUKE

Most whale behavior takes place out of sight, under water, in poor light. That is why it is hard to know many of the details of whales' lives. For example, no one has ever seen a humpback whale give birth.

Scientists have learned how to identify individual humpbacks when they surface. They recognize each whale's unique markings on its flukes and **flippers**.

When scientists see the same whale in different parts of the world, we learn about migration. When scientists identify newborns and track them as they grow, we learn about the whale's family life. We now know, for example, that fathers play no special part in bringing up their own offspring. And, there is much, much more to learn.

The unique markings on the flukes of this high-tailing humpback will allow whale scientists to find out what it eats and who it hangs with, and to track its migration.

THE HUMPBACK COMEBACK

Humpbacks start to have calves when they are young, only five years old. Also, they have one calf every two to three years. They give birth earlier and more often than other great whales. That adds up to a brighter future for humpback whales. The number of humpbacks has already started to rise.

Humans no longer legally hunt humpback whales for oil, meat, or baleen. But we are still a threat to them. Many humpbacks die in fishing nets. Many more die from collisions with ships. The greatest danger yet may be from **pollution** of the oceans.

Whale watching is a kind way to "hunt" whales, but it is best to go gently in small groups. A group of boats like this might be very disturbing to the whales.

SAVE THE OCEANS!

In 1987, fifteen humpback whales were found dead off the coast of Cape Cod. (Others may have died too, but were not found.) The Cape Cod whales had eaten mackerel full of **saxitoxin**, a poison found in **red tides**. Red tides can be caused by **sewage** that flows into the oceans from shorelines crowded with homes and businesses.

Scientists fear that the pollution, which poisons the food whales eat, also makes it hard for them to fight diseases. In recent years, dolphins, whales, and seals have died in large groups. High levels of poisons have been found in all these marine **mammals**.

If we truly want to save the whales, we need to understand and respect our oceans as a whole and protect all life in them.

A humpback lunges through a shoal of anchovies, gulping down most of them. How safe will its food be if we do not stop polluting our oceans?

MORE TO READ AND VIEW

Books (Nonfiction)
Baby Whale. Lynn Wilson (Platt & Munk)
Baby Whales Drink Milk. Barbara Juster Esbensen (Harpercollins)
Exploring the Oceans. Stephen Hall (Gareth Stevens)
Humphrey the Lost Whale. Wendy Tokuda and Richard Hall (Heian)
Ibis: A True Whale Story. John Himmelman (Scholastic)
The Whale Family Book. Cynthia D'Vincent (Picture Books Studio)
Whales and Dolphins. Victor Gentle and Janet Perry (Gareth Stevens)

Books (Fiction)
Amigo, the Friendly Gray Whale. A. Kay Lay (Waterbourne Press)
The Birth of a Humpback Whale. Robert Matero (Atheneum)
Humpback Goes North. Darice Bailer (Soundprints)
I Wonder If I'll See a Whale. Frances Ward Weller (Philomel)

Audio (Nonfiction)
Humpback Whales. Sounds of the Earth (series). (Oreade Music)

Video (Nonfiction)
Whale Adventures. (HBO)
Whale Rescue. Wildlife Tales (series). (ABC)

HUMPBACK WHALE QUICK FACTS

Average weight of adults
60,000 to 100,000 pounds (27,200 to 45,400 kg)
Females are slightly larger than males.

Average length of adults
Females: 43 feet (13.0 m)
Males: 41 feet (12.5 m)

Number of baleen
350 to 370 baleen plates, up to 3 feet (0.9 m) long

Length of life
40 to 50 years, maybe more

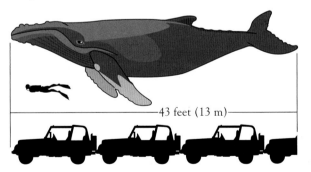

Special feature
Their flippers are a third of the length of their body — the largest for any whale.
They have knobs, called tubercles, on top of their heads, on their lower jaw, and on their flippers.

WEB SITES

If you have your own computer and Internet access, great! If not, most libraries have Internet access. The Internet changes every day, and web sites come and go. We believe the following sites are likely to last and give the best, most appropriate links for readers to find out more about the oceans, whales, and other sea life.

To get started, enter the word "museums" in a general search engine. See if you can find a museum web page that has exhibits on ocean mammals and oceanography. If any of these museums are close to home, you can visit them in person!

www.yahooligans.com
This is a huge search engine and a great research tool for anything you might want to know. For information on whales, click on Animals under the Science & Nature heading. From the Animals page, you can hear or see whales and dolphins by clicking on Animal Sounds or Animal Pictures.

Or you may want to plug some words into the search engine to see what Yahooligans can find for you. Some words related to humpback whales are *whale songs, tubercles, cetaceans,* and *red tides.*

www.whaleclub.com
The *Whale Club* is a great place to go to talk to other whale fans, talk to whale experts, and find out the latest news about whales.

www.enchantedlearning.com/
Go to Zoom School and click on Whale

Activities and Whale Dictionary for games, information sheets, and great links for many species of whales.

www.discovery.com/guides/animals/ under_water.html
Browse through information about many underwater creatures. Don't miss the topics Long-Distance Calls: Voices of the Great Whales, Humpbacks of Madagascar, and Oral History ... Straight from the Whale's Mouth. You'll read the latest information, see up-close photographs, and take amazing underwater tours.

whale.wheelock.edu
The *WhaleNet* is packed full of the latest whale research information. Some is way cool! Click on the Students and then the WhaleNet Index button to find more buttons and links that will help you find whale videos, hear echolocation, or ask a whale expert a question.

octopus.gma.org/onlocation/ali2/index.html
Meet a girl who travels around the world to study whales. Check out her latest adventure and sighting log.

GLOSSARY

You can find these words on the pages listed. Reading a word in a sentence helps you understand it even better.

baleen (buh-LEEN) — plates of fingernail-like material that hang in the mouths of some whales and strain food from sea water 8

calf (KAV) — a baby whale; plural **calves** (KAVZ) 4, 12, 18

cetaceans (sih-TAY-shuns) — members of a group of sea mammals that includes whales, dolphins, and porpoises 8

flippers (FLIP-urs) — a whale's front limbs, like a human's arms or a bird's wings 16

flukes (FLOOKS) — the two lobes forming a whale's tail 4, 16

krill (KRIL) — tiny, shrimplike animals that form very large shoals in the sea 10

mammals (MAM-uhlz) — animals that give birth to live young and feed milk to their young 20

migrate (MY-grayt) — to travel to certain places at certain times of the year 12

orcas (OR-kuhz) — also known as "killer whales" but in fact the largest kind of dolphin 4

pollution (puh-LOO-shun) — poisons put into or onto the land, air, or water 18, 20

predators (PRED-uh-turs) — animals that hunt other animals for food 4

prey (PRAY) — animals that are hunted for food 10

red tides (RED TYDZ) — an unusually strong growth of a certain tiny plant in the oceans, often caused by sewage and often turning the sea red 20

saxitoxin (sak-suh-TOK-suhn) — a poison found in red tides 20

sewage (SOO-ij) — waste materials from humans and farm animals 20

shoal (SHOHL) — a large group of fish or krill swimming together 10, 20

INDEX